Philippine Counterinsurgency Success: Implications for the Human Domain of Warfare

> Warfare centered on defeating enemies who cloak themselves in the human activity of the modern, increasingly interdependent, and virtually connected world of the 21st Century...is profoundly different from that required to dominate in the traditional Land Domain.
>
> —ADP 3-05[1]

To Influence is to Prevail

Background – The Human Domain is Defining Itself; Implications for U.S. Army Global Strategic Landpower Dominance

In its foundational doctrine publication the U.S. Army says:

> U.S. forces operate in the air, land, maritime, space and cyberspace domains. The land domain is the most complex of the domains, because it addresses humanity—its cultures, ethnicities, religions, and politics...The distinguishing characteristic of the land domain is the presence of humans in large numbers.[2]

I disagree. The distinguishing characteristics of the land domain are twofold. It is the most geographically complex domain, making it the most difficult to operate within, and it hosts the human domain, the most complex of the domains. As dissimilar as mountainous jungles are to the arctic tundra, humans have adapted to thrive in these, and other, environments. Humans are logical, thinking beings, and of the over seven billion on our planet, no two are exactly alike.

Daily human interaction occurs in many ways. Although most interaction is positive, some is not. In most instances, negative interaction is intended to modify behavior, to influence outcomes, and when coupled with a political goal and sufficient scale, it can result in war. War is unfortunately an ageless tool. Clausewitz appropriately and timelessly labeled it as "an act of violence intended to compel our enemy to fulfill our will...a continuation of political activity by other means."[3] There are various types of conflicts with unique characteristics, often only common to the time period of human history in which they occur. For that reason, "wars in every period have independent forms and independent conditions, and, therefore, every period must have its independent theory of war."[4]

This then isn't a paper about the theory of war, but about whether it is time to clearly identify the uniquely important role all people play in modern war, not just organized combatants. Further, it is time to examine whether there is a valid intersection between the concept of human security and the reality of globalization. That intersection, if you contend that today's wars have been mostly wars amongst people and not only wars between people, looks a lot like its own entity, a new domain of warfare. That domain is the human domain. And if it is indeed new and distinct from the land domain, inanimate and geographic, we in our Nation's Army should be preparing ourselves to better understand its implications. We may need to adapt how we choose to look at this operating space, how and who we train, and what it is we can capitalize on by pitting our most important resource, our Soldiers, against this newly refined task. We can accomplish this task, which thankfully, remains true to the essence of the Army's longstanding role.

As Army Chief of Staff General Raymond Odierno relates, "Direct engagement with people has always been, and remains, a core strength of the United States Army."[5] If we can optimize how we learn to better operate amongst the world's occupants in a manner that meets our national security goals, we will surely maximize the opportunity to prevent conflict between humans. As an Army, we can play our critical role in shaping the international environment to enable our partners and contain our enemies. Finally, we will be ready to win, and win decisively, by best meeting security requirements that involve close human interaction and maintain an astute understanding of today's complex world.[6]

We may never be able to accurately predict the type of war we're about to enter, but our preparations and understanding of contingencies will allow us a better understanding of its likely characteristics. Some we've seen before; some will be new. For this paper, I'll focus on war that is most common in this day and age. Today's war is most often not what we would consider traditional state-on-state, or organized army against army on well-defined battlefields. I'm not saying we won't see that again, or that's it's less likely, simply that this isn't the type of warfare most of us have recently experienced. Some would argue that this former type will regain its fashion, in particular due to increasing state capabilities and potential conflict over diminishing resources. Although we're a long way from a global order that doesn't engender nationalism by its very construct, where we'll respond to conflict and why it started are not relevant to the point of this paper. In all instances, we'll deal with human activity and more people than ever will be involved either way. I'll instead focus on what is most frequent today, war amongst the people, excellently described by General Rupert Smith as:

> a graphic description of modern warlike situations, and also a conceptual framework: it reflects the hard fact that there is no secluded battlefield upon which armies engage, nor are there necessarily armies, definitely not on all sides…war amongst the people is different: it is the reality in which the people in the streets and houses and fields-all the people, anywhere-are the battlefield.[7]

I have chosen to look at this topic from the perspective of our Army, the most agile, adaptable and capable force in the world.[8] It has always done more than our Nation expected of it, and it always will. Our Army has been expertly composed of thinking, adaptable, flexible humans from a great cross section of American society. Its doctrine empowers leadership, decision, and action down to the lowest level. Each Soldier is respected as an individual, each being crucial to the Army's success. Everyone plays a key role, important to the understanding of the concept of human security. In short, every individual is critical to the overall Army, as they always have been. So what has changed?

A Lens Through Which We're Viewed

In September of 2012 the United Nations (UN) General Assembly formally issued a statement on its common understanding for human security, a concept in discussion since the mid-1990's. Although the differentiation of the concept from the basic tenets of western liberalism continues to be debated, its fundamental points make sense particularly in light of how globalization has affected today's security environment. There are more of us on the planet, and we're closer to all being within arm's reach than we ever thought possible. In brief, the UN has articulated that people have the right "to live in freedom and dignity, free from poverty, and despair." Further, all humans are "entitled to freedom from fear and freedom from want, with an equal opportunity to enjoy all their rights and fully develop their human potential."[9]

Human security, how we coexist, has long been established and refined in the United States through the fundamental constitutional rights of every individual. These beliefs, framed from our values, are progressing globally as humanity advances, although not as evenly or quickly as we'd like to see. This is particularly important in regions of the world where the value of human life, often due to exceedingly challenging conditions and commensurate competition for limited resources, is not routinely measured by comparable ideals. The challenges humans face have always been with us, as they always will be, so the components of human security shouldn't surprise anyone and are not fundamentally different from anything we've considered in the past.[10] What does surprise many, though, is the relative size and interconnectivity of today's world, so a closer look at this concept perhaps offers us another angle from which to explore the problem, and identify its inherent opportunities.

Ideally, those particular areas where humans live, formerly physically and psychologically remote, also often potential zones of conflict and instability, will someday be prosperous regions where dignity, hope, prosperity and being content are fully manifested. We're not there yet, and as a result, the concepts of human security can have immediate implications for the employment of the strategic tools at our disposal to secure, and if required influence, those humans where they're found, whatever environment they've chosen or find themselves in. The concept of human security doesn't promote dissolution of the Westphalian state model, anarchy, or anything in between. It simply says that people, all of them, are important. The guiding points of human security, according to Canadian diplomat and leading proponent Paul Heinbecker, are that: human security takes people and their communities, rather than states, first. Human security treats the safety of people as fundamental to international peace and security and recognizes the security of Westphalian states is essential, but not sufficient to fully ensure the safety and well-being of their populations. Finally, it addresses military and non-military threats to people, and considers security as a continuum.[11] Thankfully, through positive international steps like establishment of the United Nations with its commensurate conventions and fundamental declarations of human rights, Geneva conventions and protocols, as well as an interconnected world that can globally process information seconds after events, the importance of human security is more broadly recognized and understood. Although not important to all the world's armies, it's important to our Army.

Unfortunately, though, that recognition and understanding has yet to manifest itself in all of us getting along, and that fact has not driven a subsequent decrease in the propensity or frequency for overall global violence. For the foreseeable future the world will remain a violent place. That includes not only regular violence between states, but irregular violence, that which is "ever more lethal, capable of producing widespread chaos, and otherwise difficult to counter…enmeshed in the population and increasingly empowered by astute use of communications, cyberspace, and technology…essentially contests for influence and legitimacy over relevant populations."[12] What does change, though, is what a large portion of the world sees through the lens of human security and increased rights of individuals, combined with globalization and near-immediate wide-scale human interconnectivity. Those elements indicate that modern military operations, especially war, have become exceedingly complex. In fact, they've become so complex in crowded human space that an independent domain of operational consideration has likely arisen. Although it has existed forever as an entity, its importance in today's international security environment, that inherent complexity, and the fact that it remains at the root of all conflict as well as holds the keys to peace, has caused the requirement for an evolution in how we view it. That entity is of course the human domain. How then will we seek to function within this human domain while accomplishing objectives that ensure human security? Can we do it, or do we simply assume that force-on-force operations, even as they continue to evolve in definition, will be a sufficient focus to help guide us through today's security environment?

New Focus on the Core Issue

The United States possesses tremendous strategic capability that is often associated with an international requirement to put it to use to the positive benefit of the global community. A component of that capability is the military instrument of national power, one often used to help ensure human security by addressing the incredibly numerous threats that inhibit positive human interaction. Never especially prescient at predicting where those would come from next--a near impossibility--it has however been good at adapting and meeting its requirements as the military component of U.S. policy objectives. That force has been useful throughout the history of our nation, providing that there is "an understanding of the political context of the operation, and the role of the military within it. Only when adaptation and context are complete can force be applied with utility."[13]

Within that world-class military, land forces, principally our Army, and to a certain extent also our Marine Corps, have the principal responsibility of accomplishing tasks on land. Operating on land is multi-faceted, constantly changing, and subsequently requires unified action, "the synchronization, coordination, and/or integration of the activities of governmental and nongovernmental entities within military operations to achieve unity of effort."[14] To win against humans, you must meet or influence them in their environment, and all components must work in close concert, synchronized with all the available capabilities. Similarly, land forces will predominate actions within the human domain, although other components of the joint force may also play their necessary critical role, whether in support, or in some instances, in the lead. After all, this is about humans interacting with other humans, so requirement and best option, not the type of uniformed service represented, will drive recommended solution.

7

Land has obviously long been the domain of human beings, and it goes without saying that we humans remain peerless in our ability to complicate interaction within that domain. In fact, through globalization we can do so much more comprehensively and quickly today than at any time before. More of us equals more complexity and competition for limited resources. To address that complexity, military operations on land, similar to other domains, have evolved over time with the changing characteristics of warfare. The most adaptable of those land-centric militaries, the United States Army, has always provided our Nation its landpower prowess, defined as, "the ability—by threat, force, or occupation—to gain, sustain, and exploit control over land, resources, and people."[15] That complexity is greatly magnified by the requirement to influence humans, forcing us to seek balance in the confluence of land operations within the human domain. Those land operations within the human domain take on increased significance as a result of their specific purpose, that of human influence, subsequently elevating them to the level of strategic landpower. If specific to the requirement to operate within the human domain, strategic landpower can indeed prevent, shape, and win in whatever volatile, complex, uncertain, and ambiguous environment it finds itself. In fact, if we truly capture its essence, we'll likely be better prepared to win by not fighting. In today's world, actions performed by few are seen by many. We must ensure those strategic effects continue to work in our favor.

Our Nation's force of strategic landpower, the Army, is "the most powerful deterrent to aggression against U.S. interests worldwide, and its dominance must remain unquestioned. Strategic landpower results from possessing unequalled capacity in both human and land domains."[16] Human behavior, whether state or non-state, is warfare's millennia-old object of influence. Sun Tzu, the Chinese theorist of war, wrote more than 2,000 years ago, "The supreme art of war is to subdue the enemy without fighting."[17] However, if a force must fight to physically ensure that influence, then "the only geography that can really be controlled is the only geography that lends itself physically to human occupation, the land…it is the very character of land warfare to hold at risk…civil society…."[18] Simply put, land forces operating amongst humans seeking to effect change in their behavior are forces of strategic landpower.

Although the objective remains unchanged, the arsenal of tools at landpower's disposal has evolved and can generally be organized into word or deed categories. War has both physical and psychological dimensions that allow employing forces to compel and lead enemies and non-combatants to act.[19] The degree to which those tools can yield a power that produces effect, either desired or unintended, determines when and how they are employed. When employing strategic landpower amongst people, it remains paramount to act and to assist appropriate elements of the international community committed to "an international order that promotes just peace."[20] As a result, strategic landpower forces must understand the myriad implications for human security within that human domain in which they've been sent to act. Those implications constantly evolve through refined acceptable responsibilities that protect all human life, understandable to a force of strategic landpower. This evolution is particularly important and beneficial for the vast majority of humans directly impacted by military interaction, non-combatants, and one of the primary reasons why there is now a human domain.

Why is Today any Different from Yesterday?

Ever since the dawn of armed conflict, non-combatants have constituted a growing majority grouping of humans within a particular operating area. Armies and navies left from, passed through, and arrived at points on a map that contained a human population. Perhaps they fought on fields of battle, debatable only if that field was your walled city, against a comparable component of force that sought advantage in the particular domain. Armies fought armies; navies fought navies; and those domains, extensions of human activity, were essentially what defined the requirement for warfare. As a result, when conflicts took place, usually, civilian casualties were mostly incidental to action. To defeat the field army was sufficient influence to attain a political outcome against the greater whole. There were prolonged periods of time when the expectation of force-on-force violence was commensurately as high as the requirement to protect civilians. The military purpose, per se, was to prevail over an opponent in whatever domain he occupied. Forces of invention and technology, and subsequently their ability to multiply the scope and scale of violence, increased greatly, and as a result there arose instances of great human suffering and tragedy that overflowed the bounds of uniformed combatants, in particular beginning with the Spanish Civil War and culminating with World War II.

The fields and walls that once held conflict no longer do. Indiscriminate bombings, with regard to legal combatants, of civilian population centers are but one example of how things have changed. As a result, the international community responded with legal and humanitarian requirements reminding us of the expectation that those types of conflicts should not happen again. Although the tragedy was too great, it did in a sense bring forth some positive results. The horrors of that conflict did

10

serve to legally improve protections for non-combatants, as well as develop legal safeguards to ensure many inhumane elements of technology were not incorporated into warfare's arsenal. To that point, the domain of warfare, as it was principally force on force, was where that force was found. Battle was taken to the enemy, either to terrain he wanted, or to his army, a manifestation of his power. There are many great examples, and Napoleon's campaigns are but some examples of how it was quite effectively done. However, here we begin to see how his conditions were different than today's, and why our understanding should adapt to that difference. To put it into perspective, Napoleon's armies marched on a planet of approximately one billion humans, individuals mostly armed with farm implements unless they had a closely controlled weapon assigned by their state, lived in the United States, or carried a bow, spear, rock, or knife.

Today, there are approximately seven billion people on earth, many of whom possess some type of personal firearm. It is estimated that there are now upward of 500 million small arms worldwide, 100 million which are Kalashnikov variants.[21] The complexities of operating on land continue to reflect the complexities of human life on our planet. Add to that increased number of weapons ubiquitous long-range communications tools and mechanisms, near-instant visual imaging and their commensurate worldwide interconnectivity, and the friction of human competition, and the sense of that complexity begins to come into focus. With more humans and urbanization, the ability to hide in plain sight has exponentially grown. As a result, human combatants now often have to be dealt with individually, as do non-combatants through human security principles, which when combined with those challenges and effects of globalization sheds further light on the human domain.

Following the last great global conflict of 1939-1945, forces quickly emerged to change the geometry of the post-colonial world. One of the resulting characteristics is that conflicts seem to be more and more localized, causing civilians to be more and more within the fray of violence. Separating friend from foe, combatant from non-combatant, while rightly remaining within the legal bounds of international law and appropriate moral and ethical values, has become more complicated. The days of armed combatants wearing brightly colored uniforms, a fair amount of brass, feathered hats and pom poms on their shoes are likely behind us. In fact, many of today's combatants don't wear uniforms at all, may only be combatants part time or for a few minutes, and use one of those hundreds of millions of readily available global small arms. That complexity, confusion in the ranks, and frankly lack of or difficulty of reaching an opponent now means in many instances civilian casualties are deliberate and intended for effect. They have become the interlocutor of previously organized formations, doing the bidding for themselves. In fact, "as internal armed conflicts proliferate, civilians have become the principal victims."[22] Recent examples abound, from Srebrenica in Bosnia, to the atrocities of Mozambique, Rwanda, and Sudan, where the vast majority of casualties were civilian.[23]

Fortunately, most states don't set off to target civilians specifically, but the forces of conflict within states can be, once released, difficult to control. Look no further than Syria, where of this writing, over 40,000 people have been killed, most of whom never wore a uniform or intended to participate in war prior to being drawn in or caught in the crossfire of violent conflict. So, although humans today are as important as they've ever been, they are playing a more central role to the dialogue of warfare, whether as combatants or non-combatants. More wars, mostly internal, combined with a growing human population, means more humans are involved. This means we can ill afford to look at humans as occupying terrain, water, or air as an objective of influence; we have to look at humans themselves as the terrain. Human security, in a more densely packed and subsequently smaller world, requires a human domain approach to how we operate.

However, with increasing complexity also come opportunities. In this case, we can continue to excel at meeting our Nation's security objectives, while better ensuring we respect and defend human security and contend with the increasing number of humans in and around where landpower must operate. Strategic landpower can thrive in the human domain by tailoring its focus from the terrain to what is most strategic, the human population. In fact, to this end, applying less of what is more suited may in the end be more appropriate. Our goal should then be for the right humans, properly enabled, to engage for maximum influence the right humans.

A broader understanding of, and strategic approach towards, humans doesn't mean that we intend to be all things to all people. It should however mean that when we operate, we should continue to do it right. By being more specifically right, we can have great effect. To that end, the concept of human security is not simply synonymous with the doctrine of responsibility to protect. The human security concept posits that freedom from fear is a fundamental right of every human being, every day of his or her life. Responsibility to protect is a perspective governing how states must protect their populations from "avoidable catastrophe...but when they are unwilling or unable to do so, that responsibility must be borne by the broader community of states."[24] Where we are applied is up to our policy leaders on behalf of the American people. It does however remain our job to provide options on how we can best operate to achieve the desired effect we're intended to have. That effect will always involve humans, and operations within the human domain are paramount, as well as being the most complex. By refining, as needed, application of strategic landpower for any challenges to our collective security interests we can present more policy options to minimize conflict and attain positive outcomes.

A Human Domain Operational Success

The Republic of the Philippines is a recent successful model of the inherent understanding of the human domain of warfare, as well as an example of positive application of an understanding of how that domain is critical to the responsibility to protect and enforce human security. The Philippines has closely examined the concept of human security within the human domain in the modern era, mid-stride in the conduct of a long-standing military campaign, and effected a positive operational change based upon a clearer understanding of what was needed. In short, they made it work. They were able to adapt; they had the right people; they were able to evolve their approach while under tremendous pressure to succeed, while retaining the positives from prior approaches in which they'd dedicated almost 30 years of struggle.

The former operating environment of the Armed Forces of the Republic of the Philippines was a combination of the domains of land, water, and air. For decades, they put their implements of war to use, in a traditional sense, across these domains. They fought hard for, and controlled, key terrain, patrolled sea lanes of communication, and

14

conducted amphibious and air assault operations, as well as provided close air support for troops in contact. Recently, that construct changed. They began to better focus on the people, the human domain, and as a result are now winning their internal struggles.

Evolution of Approach

The approximately 7,200-island archipelago of the Philippines has struggled for cohesive independence since Ferdinand Magellan perished by a Filipino sword on her shores in 1521. Despite that initial tactical defensive success by an indigenous warrior, the modern-day Philippines has been greatly influenced by nearly 350 years of challenging Spanish occupation followed by the United States' only colonial experience, also an era marked with extended periods of intense conflict and strife. The sole Spanish-American interlude prior to independence was during Japanese occupation, itself bringing tremendous turmoil with residual effects to the archipelago. Following American liberation from Imperial Japan, the Republic of the Philippines gained its complete independence on July 4th, 1946. This unyielding external influence on the entire archipelago did not engender optimal conditions for internal stability and the unifying cohesion necessary to maximize the tremendous talents of her extremely diverse population. Those alien external factors, combined with myriad internal divisions as the country struggled to find her feet post-World War II independence, only increased the volatility of interaction between fiercely independent peoples of different ethnic, cultural, and religious backgrounds. The post-World War II Philippine government has been no stranger to internal conflict, whether from communists, separatists, religious extremists, or from itself. To that end, its experience is worth understanding, in general terms, to glean possible lessons, particularly as it seems the

15

current Aquino administration has likely turned a corner toward success and lasting peace.

The Government of the Philippines (GPH) has literally faced decades of multiple, persistent conflicts that have given it the opportunity, as a learning and adaptive democratically-elected institution, to formulate an effective strategy and approach for internal stability. This approach, much improved over time through tremendous effort, trial and error, and near-constant United States support since 1946, must be pertinent to any observer interested in how modern-day democracies conduct effective counterinsurgency operations. Strategies and mechanisms, possibly effective in the unique scenarios of past conflicts, are no longer feasible or acceptable to either modern internal populations or today's international community. The application of central governance to a vast archipelago is especially difficult without a solid foundation of good governance. Respective islands, sometimes closely formed within regions, sometimes uniquely independent, become over time unique microcosms of human interaction. Without a solid common foundation towards greater good, they can become isolated from each other and cause uniquely challenging security situations to evolve.

What is acceptable, and likely the key to Philippines' counterinsurgency success, is that it experienced a strategic change in perspective to its modern counterinsurgency approach, a change that evolved as the seemingly endless conflict, principally against a Muslim insurgency in the southern Philippines, continued. Although the Philippines has faced a challenge from a communist insurgency since its independence, traditional counterinsurgency approaches, to include the passage of time, as well as broad-scale societal reintegration policies, the inexorable expansion of good governance, and a mismatch of communist ideology to the Filipino experiences, have all led to the remaining small number of communist ideologues to be more interested in personal financial profit through crime and extortion than their Maoist struggle. That said, communist insurgents as well as another much more prevalent type of armed faction, Private Armed Groups (PAGs), challenged by current Filipino law but extremely difficult to police, continue to muddy the security waters. Coincidentally, the communist counterinsurgency experience model was directly translated to the Muslim insurgency to be discussed in greater detail, with limited effect.

Over time, and largely proven ineffective at eliminating root causes and decreasing the number of armed combatants, the Armed Forces of the Philippines (AFP), by applying broader GPH support, found an approach that works in this much more demanding human environment, the domain of Muslim Filipinos. Beyond merely focusing on separating insurgents of various stripes from the local population, and more specifically terrorists from insurgents and the local population, a near impossibility in the southern Philippines due to many factors, the AFP served to change the angle of the lens from which a comprehensive GPH approach could protect its population. This protection, a principle tenet to the recent Internal Peace and Security Plan – Bayanihan, evolved beyond a current understanding of the inherent difficulty of what dealing with a complex internal religious insurgency must be like. To the GPH, the population is now much more than an unconcerned bystander to an internal force-on-force scenario. As a former Philippine Western Mindanao Command (WESMINCOM) Commanding General (CG) most clearly stated, "we're not at war with our own people," a critical but often seemingly overlooked point in counterinsurgency.[25]

The population, humans, became the domain in an archipelago of islands, water, and air space, within which the security forces had to operate. Unlike one of the approaches used against the communist New People's Army, population relocation was not an option. Muslims have long lived in the Philippines and with indigenous Filipino peoples possess significant claims to ancestral domains. The overall strategy of the GPH then owes its success to its ability to influence the long-term behavior of all elements of its society, whether they are insurgents, support the insurgency, are uncommitted, or support the government. Governments must govern, generally through the will of their populations who consent to governance, and as a result their behavior enables that governance to flourish. So in essence the mechanism for the GPH to prevail in its long-standing counterinsurgency operations was to protect its entire population, supportive or non-supportive, from itself by operating for it, and within its midst where its projection of national intent was most needed. They needed to be seen as having the ability to govern, to make a difference, and to be an acceptable control mechanism to a formerly ignored population hundreds of miles south and thousands of islands away from Manila. The focus of the GPH then became its people, not its geography, causing a natural evolution from the formerly unsuccessful physical domain-centric approach to what makes their government required and feasible, its human population. They entered into and operated within the human domain.

More than simply looked at as terrain to maneuver over, through, or around, the human population was essentially viewed as an operational domain in and of itself. The GPH reflected on the population through a series of lenses, including physical, social, demographic, religious, multi-cultural, indigenous, settled, and psychological issues. As a result, and certainly not without understanding of the tremendous complexity, the GPH strategically served to immerse itself in the element that, until essentially the past five years, had been at best misunderstood, and at worst, ignored due to myriad historical factors. A few strategic schools of thought, perhaps led by one that believed remote populations could be ignored, conveniently allowed the central government to principally focus on the mainland of Luzon, while successive bands of influence decreased until, separated by different culture, language, and importantly religion, the extreme southern reaches of the Philippines fell somewhere between being ignored and tolerated; both clearly unacceptable. This intolerance and focus on differences, easier to justify in an archipelago than contiguous land mass, naturally fit with the southern Philippines Moro belief that they were essentially independent of the central authority, through a false narrative lore of never having been fully conquered by the Spanish, Americans, or the Filipino Tagalogs of Luzon. Fundamentally, the current President Benigno Aquino administration developed a new paradigm of thought that envisioned successful ways, allowing for increased strategic options towards progress despite the requirement to meet a time-critical end before the completion of his constitutionally mandated one term administration.

Although the initial cause of the Muslim insurgency is not as important now as it once was, in particular considering changes in perspective over the four-plus decade struggle, it remains relevant to the mosaic of conflict and may now serve to identify where opportunities that were once lost have since been gained.

The Perils of Ignoring the Human Domain

The catalyst marking the beginning of the modern era of counterinsurgency in the Philippines post-independence was the result of an incident on Corregidor when Muslim

19

Filipinos, known as Moros since the period of Spanish occupation, were killed by their Armed Forces of the Philippines comrades, an act which the GPH unsuccessfully tried to cover up. This event, combined with long-standing grievances against central government authority, led to the formation of the Moro National Liberation Front (MNLF). In 1970 the MNLF began openly fighting the GPH, itself at that time well involved in a communist insurgency further north in the archipelago. Although a nominal peace accord was reached with the primary group in 1976, following thousands of casualties on both sides, a more fundamental splinter group, the Moro Islamic Liberation Front (MILF), arose and continued to oppose the GPH. It should be noted during this era U.S. support to the Philippines remained significant, with massive presence at Clark Air Base and Subic Bay Naval Base, although primarily focused on U.S. operations in Southeast Asia. Many U.S. counterinsurgency tactics, techniques, and procedures from Viet Nam were shared with our Filipino allies, principally through the Joint U.S. Military Assistance Group Philippines, and those were adapted and applied by Filipino practitioners, some of whom had themselves served as either insurgents or counterinsurgents during the Japanese occupation of 1941-1945.

This approach did not work, resulting in force-on-force operations against Moro insurgents essentially continuing unabated throughout the 1970s and 1980s. With no end seemingly in sight, a temporary political solution to essentially isolate the broader issues was attempted in 1989, marked by President Corazon Aquino's negotiated settlement with the MNLF establishing the Autonomous Region of Muslim Mindanao. This grasp at a lasting solution was followed by a more binding peace agreement with the central government in 1996. The Autonomous Region of Muslim Mindanao

(ARMM), a combined central government and insurgent group attempt at directly addressing the principle grievance of lack of good governance, has predictably been a failure. The International Crisis Group succinctly provides its opinion of the ARMM's failure in noting that the characteristics of the ARMM included abuse of power, violence, and crime as intrinsic to the politics of Mindanao and the Sulu archipelago. They also called it an unmitigated disaster, and a venal and corrupt entity that has no power over the warlords-cum-politicians who, in the past, Manila chose to pit against the MILF. So unworthy was this sub-state solution to its population that the International Crisis Group concluded that "this failed autonomous region, which exists to this day, has obstructed the search for a political solution to the Muslim insurgency."[26]

Despite attaining some of its political goals through establishment of the ARMM, not the least of which was gaining maneuver space through time, the insurgency continued unabated as the MILF continued its operations against the GPH, shifting grievances and causes as needed to maintain its relative power. The instability created by these insurgent groups proved fertile ground for nascent terrorist organizations, compounding the challenges faced by the GPH and increasing the pressure, soon to be international, to attain a lasting solution. The most infamous of these internal terrorist nodes, the Abu Sayyaf Group (ASG), was formed in 1990 from Filipino jihadists returning from Afghanistan and Pakistan. This violent group, capitalizing on funding from its own terrorist activities and al Qaeda (AQ) support through Jemaah Islamiyah (JI), the Indonesian-based regional AQ affiliate, served to maximize the complexity of the challenge to the GPH. Sadly, the Philippines had become a major terrorist operational planning and training location, one which produced several thousand

21

regional jihadists from southern Philippine terrorist training camps. These terrorist groups appropriately believed the southern islands presented a territorial safe haven containing a supportive human infrastructure required for their sustenance, and subsequent expansion.

The same factors also serve to illustrate the commensurate operational environment for the GPH. The ideological founder of the ASG was eventually killed by GPH authorities in 1998; however, his brother's ascension to a leadership role only drove the group to more violent acts, such as the March 2000 kidnapping of a Priest, teachers, and students, numbering nearly 50 individuals, from the island of Basilan. One month later, the ASG terrorists internationalized their objective by kidnapping tourists from a Malaysian island, which led President Arroyo to seek U.S. military assistance to train a response force. Libyan intervention brought an end to this particular incident, in exchange for $20 million in funding to the terrorists, which they immediately put to use for additional operational acts. On the GPH side and with U.S. Special Forces support, training began for a nascent military counter-terror capability that would specifically be known as the Light Reaction Company. The following month, the ASG again struck, this time on the Philippines' Palawan Island, kidnapping hostages from a resort, three of whom were Americans. One of the Americans was almost immediately killed, while another was killed in a subsequent rescue attempt.

The events of September 11, 2001 strengthened the combined Philippine-U.S. resolve to act, a decision that led to more direct U.S. support, eventually in the form of a joint special operations task force enabling U.S. forces to support GPH counter-terror efforts. A U.S. State Department message of the time correctly reported:

U.S. counterterrorism efforts also expanded beyond the borders of Afghanistan in 2002, with operations in the Philippines, Georgia, and Yemen. Early in the year, 1,200 advisors were dispatched to the Philippines to train soldiers fighting members of the radical Islamist group Abu Sayyaf.... Following the conclusion of training in July, several hundred U.S. soldiers remained in the Philippines to assist with infrastructure projects.[27]

United States Pacific Command (USPACOM) assumed the mission, and its Special Operations Command Pacific and the 1st Special Forces Group (Airborne) conducted an initial assessment on the island of Basilan that indicated "the AFP did not view the population as the center of gravity, abuses were not uncommon, and corruption was endemic. In addition, AFP tactics were based on maneuver of battalion-sized forces that were often unable to find and close with terrorists on the island."[28] They did not view the human domain as worthy of consideration for comprehensive operations. Although the initial U.S. concept was to train and advise GPH forces on the island of Basilan, the mission eventually evolved to its modern form, which is the conduct of foreign internal defense in support of comprehensive GPH efforts to defeat violent extremist organizations. Advisory assistance provided to the AFP since 2002, although principally focused on specific terrorist groups, enabled broader applicability in military functions such as professionalization initiatives, understanding of human rights and international humanitarian law, logistical support, and effective management of tactical enablers. The U.S. – Filipino partnership has allowed for tremendous operational success, while the strategic evolution of the overall campaign design for the Philippines has been uniquely Filipino, and uniquely successful. The Philippines changed its approach first by examining the fundamental requirements of human security and how they were the critical component of understanding, and operating within, the human domain.

23

Evolution of Filipino Strategy – Focus on Human Domain by Understanding and Applying Human Security Doctrine

Since 2002, U.S. military forces, as a component of a comprehensive U.S. interagency effort, have directly supported the Philippine military and police, particularly focused on the Government of the Philippine's counter-terrorism efforts within the authorities allowed by the Philippine constitution. Although understanding the tremendous challenges of both their communist and Islamic insurgencies, U.S. military support since 2001 has been directed at assisting the GPH in eliminating a terrorist threat that sought opportunity from this chaotic internal environment. The combined efforts of both governments have been successful in degrading the capabilities of regionally inspired terrorist groups, principally JI and the ASG, and have neutralized their ability to operate cohesively beyond the immediate region. According to the Congressional Research Service, "Joint military activities have reduced the numbers of terrorist fighters in the South…[diminished] Abu Sayyaf's strength and presence, [and]…the ASG's leadership core reportedly has been reduced by about three-fourths."[29] That said, the evolution of the current process has not been without challenges, many of which were only recently overcome by a shift in strategy made possible by their new focus on human security within the human domain, articulated by the public issuance of the Internal Peace and Security Plan – Bayanihan. For example, the International Crisis Group attempted to articulate concerns of the prior strategy as an effort by U.S. forces to strengthen the military of the Philippines using "civic action," which would serve to isolate rebels from the Muslim populace, going on to report that "if their goal is to defeat the ASG and its foreign, mainly Indonesian, jihadi allies, they are casting the net too widely and creating unnecessary enemies." Their continued

24

assessment is that mass-based insurgencies such as the Muslim MILF and MNLF versions rely on supportive populations, and that by "extension, small numbers of terrorists rely on sympathetic insurgents…counter-terrorism's central task in a setting like the one found in the Philippines is to isolate jihadis from their insurgent hosts – not divide insurgents from the population." Finally, in its closing argument, the report states:

> This has come at a heavy price in Sulu, where no equivalent ceasefire machinery exists to separate jihadis from the dominant local guerrilla force, the Moro National Liberation Front (MNLF). Instead, heavy-handed offensives against ASG and its foreign jihadi allies have repeatedly spilled over into MNLF communities, driving some insurgents into closer cooperation with the terrorists, instead of with government.[30]

Clearly not working, this approach was completely overhauled in stride, along with continued fundamental security sector reform that addressed the paradox of the Armed Forces of the Philippines responsibility for internal security, in lieu of territorial defense and overall national sovereignty, while the Philippine National Police was struggling with separating itself from localized politics and the archaic selection method for police leadership. Local politicians, sometimes not necessarily in concert with national government strategy, have been known to employ elements of the local police force as a political enforcement mechanism instead of as a required entity to ensure the maintenance of peace and order, one which is seen to protect and defend its population. They select, and deselect, local police chiefs at will. Transparency International provides a telling indicator by ranking the Philippines as 105th of 176 nations and territories in its 2012 Corruption Perceptions Index, keeping close company in the rankings with Mexico, Mali, and Algeria. Despite these challenges, both the AFP and Philippine National Police have made much progress, a great deal of it following their change of perspective toward human security and the human domain.

25

Effective January 1, 2011, the AFP shifted its internal peace and security campaign to focus on the human domain and clearly articulated it in an open document entitled the Internal Peace and Security Plan "Bayinahan" (IPSP). Although a military plan, President Benigno S. Aquino III provided the opening message to the document and stated that "the ills confronting our nation are multi-faceted and complex. These can never be addressed through raising arms and wielding force against our democratic way of life as a nation. In the same vein, we recognize that a purely military solution will never be enough to adequately address the issues."[31] The plan reinforces the mandate that the primary duty of the Philippine government is to protect its population and articulates the principal role of the Armed Forces of the Philippines is as the protector of the people and state. The plan addresses the continued necessity for a whole-of-nation approach, beyond whole-of-government, to come to terms with and address the factors that lead to insurgency, "structural problems in Philippine society, such as unequal development, non-delivery of basic services, injustice, and poor governance—all of which are beyond the military's purview."[32] This is a critical concept and the reason it becomes one of the two foundational approaches in the plan.

The government indeed plays a critical role in the success of this strategy, but it cannot do so without the inclusion and support of the public sector. As a result, the entire nation is in effect trying to reach a solution to its own problems. Coincidentally, the second foundational approach is that of protecting the population, again directly related to the human domain. In fact, in the background of the IPSP, the AFP provides an early sense of perspective and how it will apply to security sector operations: "There is therefore a need for the military institution to re-imagine the concept of security to one

26

that embraces a broader view of human security. Assuming the wider concept of

human security will allow the AFP to assume a support role in the nation building efforts

of the national government, subservient to the theme of peace and development."[33]

This broader view of human security addresses the consideration of the human domain.

By extension, the desired strategic endstate became the well-being of the population.

That well-being of the population, earned from successful operations in the human

domain, would then result in the stability of state institutions. Stable state institutions in

turn then better enable the defense of territorial integrity, a core AFP mission, which

serves to ensure the protection of sovereignty, a strategic focal point for the nation in

light of territorial issues in the South China Sea. In short, this strategic change has

allowed the AFP to better focus on its core task of protecting its nation, by protecting its

population.

From that desired strategic end state, human well being, the GPH articulated four

key elements of its National Strategic Policy, the ways in which it will attain its strategic

end state: governance, delivery of basic services, economic reconstruction, and

sustainable development and security sector reform. The means used to attain those

ways come from a "whole-of-nation" approach, essentially a whole-of-government effort

supported by private sector, and one which is "people-centered," focused on the human

domain. Within the plan, elements of the public and private sector are assigned tasks

representing the key components of the strategy. One of the strategic ways to attain

objectives in the security sector reform category was to assign the Department of

National Defense the task of defense and security. The IPSP is subsequently that department's articulation of the national requirement, which conceptually captured the broader stakeholder involvement necessitated in all states of its creation.

As stated by the AFP, the IPSP is a shared, co-owned, and co-authored document with a planning horizon of 2011 to 2016. The plan is clearly focused on winning the peace. As President Aquino stated during a 2010 AFP Change of Command ceremony, "the military functions best when both the military and civilian leadership share a clear and common understanding what is national security, and accordingly, what threatens it...further emphasizing that national security objectives must be focused on protecting human rights and civil liberties."[34] Here the essence of the strategy is clearly articulated. The paradigm shift of the IPSP is acknowledgment of the broader role of human security, understanding that security is intended to protect first the people of the state and then the state, and that comprehensive military operations must keep those principles in mind by the balanced application of kinetic and non-kinetic actions.

The mission of the AFP for internal peace and security, from this strategy, then becomes to "conduct support operations to win the peace in order to help the Filipino nation create an environment conducive for sustainable development and a just and lasting peace."[35] The intended result of the strategy is long term and is viewed through a lens of how military operations affect the people and their communities. The operating space is no longer territorial, which was disproven as a suitable strategy, and becomes in effect within the human domain, through the population. The first underpinning strategic approach is the entire nation must focus its collective efforts on behalf of a comprehensive solution. The second is that this focus must be its people, their human domain. Finally, under the whole-of-nation approach, it is seen as critical that all citizens, not just government employees, are active participants in the pursuit of their own peace and security. This in essence creates a shared concept and overall understanding of what constitutes security.

Under the people-centered perspective, the human domain emerges: "People's welfare is at the center of military operations, primacy of their human rights drives operations, and it promotes local security and safety based on the needs and realities of communities."[36] In its most basic articulation of the importance of peoples' welfare, human security is defined as "freedom from fear and freedom from want. It is the state of being able to live with human dignity. More than the absence of violent conflict, human security means the protection and respect for human rights, good governance..."[37] It is clear the essence of the IPSP focus has shifted to the human domain, not simply on defeating the threat, or simply stated as protecting the population. The plan clearly articulates a human domain approach, and within the frame of human security, "puts peoples' welfare at the center of its operations...primacy to human rights and also explores ways on promoting local security and safety based on the needs and realities of communities on the ground."[38]

An acute example of the success of human domain operations occurred on the Philippine island of Basilan in early 2012. Following a violent large-scale engagement in which nearly two dozen soldiers and an unknown number of civilians were killed, GPH efforts, personally led by President Aquino, effectively placed the onus on the population to determine the best response to the incident by strictly adhering to rule of law and employing a novel, human-centric approach. In nationally broadcast comments, President Aquino articulated that first and foremost, rule of law was important to the continued progress of the Philippines. He declared that individuals acting outside of that rule would be subject to arrest by the national police. What insurgents had done to AFP soldiers was first and foremost a crime and would be addressed as such. Finally, he stated that warrants would be appropriately generated under the Filipino legal framework. He termed this approach "all out justice" and it very quickly resonated with the population.

For the first time in countering the insurgency specific negative actors were identified and essentially isolated from law-abiding citizens by indirect influence. The population was specifically informed of who was wanted by police, why they were wanted, what crimes they were suspected of having committed, and as a result how they were accused of having broken Philippine law. Furthermore, it was quickly understood that they would get their day in court, unique from the longstanding wanted poster approach that mostly unsuccessfully pitted family member against family member. Almost immediately, tip lines began to receive more data enabling police forces to begin more specific and judicious operations within the human domain. As a result, numerous wanted criminals lost their ability to hide in plain sight amongst a neutral population and several were soon apprehended. Families felt more comfortable providing data on relatives because their faith in the legal system would provide justice.

Prior approaches, mostly unsuccessful, were for additional military forces to temporally saturate the area of contact and try to capture insurgents. Most often, none would be found, nor would locals feel free to support AFP efforts. The pattern of violence was therefore propagated by a failure to understand the nuances of how to best persistently operate within the domain in order to attain results through appropriate dominance of its key terrain, those insurgents who seemingly always lived to fight another day.

Implications for U.S. Strategic Landpower

We must recognize the human domain as principle and seek to understand its implications to how we operate. We ignore how the world has changed at our peril. These gradual and generational changes of thought, concepts, technology, and globalization, have caused us to reach the tipping point of physical domain-centric thought. We must be prepared to influence within the human domain in as timely a manner as possible, either to deter conflict or quickly contain and eliminate it. We have reached the point where humans, all of them within an operating area, are much more than terrain, whether key or not. This change in perception and thought is fundamental, not nuanced, and as a result brings forth certain implications for the future that we must examine. That examination should be done in a comprehensive, detailed, but timely manner to ensure we're ready for operations and will not miss an opportunity. Fortunately, the Army and U.S. Special Operations Command have identified this requirement and are moving forward with a combined body to explore strategic landpower. One of its focus areas will clearly be the human domain.

An initial task of the Office for Strategic Landpower should be to harmonize the efforts of the human domain communities of interest and analyze these implications. We must truly study the components, physical and psychological, of human domain and adapt as necessary to apply the Army's perfectly suited core competencies to address our roles and missions. We should look at our doctrine and whether we have the proper organization to adapt. We must determine if we regionally align units towards locales,

31

populations, or both. We should decide how to adapt our training to meet the demands of human domain operations by balancing the focus even more towards human factors like culture and communications mechanisms such as language and tools, psychology, and anthropological skills. We need to identify how our leaders prepare to function across the human domain and how we apply mission command to volatile, uncertain, complex, and ambiguous environments. We must identify how we get ourselves to where we need to be in order to best influence outcomes, to include better applying the tools we have and likely developing new ones that allow us to operate within areas, blend in, influence from within or afar, develop and maintain understanding, and better deal with humans. We should determine how we recruit the right talent and where it comes from within our own population and whether current recruitment practices allow us to meet projected human domain operational requirements. Finally, we must determine whether we're in the right places to influence the human domain. Are we properly arrayed, are we in the right bases, and are we postured to be in the right place at the right time to capitalize on opportunity?

Our Nation will retain its global role, one that benefits all Americans. Globalization is upon us, and its full effects remain unknown. As stated in *Joint Operating Environment 2010*, "The developed world recognizes that is has a major stake in the continuing progress of globalization...Nevertheless, one should not ignore the histories and passions of popular opinion in these states as they make their appearance.... A more peaceful, cooperative world is possible only if the pace of globalization continues."[39] We must know if understanding of the human domain, how globalization and human security have met, will force us to make doctrinal, organizational, and equipment changes.

Conclusion

Our joint doctrine reminds us domains are interdependent. In a period of more focused resources, we should also examine whether we can focus our military doctrine to match those resources. As the human domain is the intersection of domains, a start is to focus there. As we are the force of strategic landpower, our risks towards not properly aiming that focus may be irrelevance at best, and mission failure at worst.

As our Nation's Army, we are the force of choice for and can accomplish our Nation's military objectives by properly employing the tools of strategic landpower. Our Army remains "unique in its capability to deliver strategic effect through the taking and exercise of control" and uniquely suited to the exigencies of that task. We remain unique in our role, in that "no other grand strategic instrument, military or nonmilitary, can achieve a similar effect."[40] Properly trained, employed, and with a deep understanding of the myriad complexities of operating within the human domain, U.S. strategic landpower can attain all objectives it seeks to attain in support of our National interests while maintaining the fundamental requirements of human security. Many types of operations involve considerations of operating in the human domain. Those include how to be precise in the use of force, empathy, cultural understanding while working alongside partner forces to support their objectives, the use of all mechanisms of a unified action approach, and operations through a comprehensive multi-lateral and interagency manner. U.S. strategic landpower is adaptable, flexible and solution-based. It is well prepared to anticipate and meet operational requirements of international perspectives on human security that seek to require "people-centered, comprehensive, context-specific and prevention-oriented responses that strengthen the protection and empowerment of all people and all communities."[41] People-centered and protection are concepts we've long understood, and with a clear understanding of the importance and true essence of the human domain, we enhance our flexibility and subsequently our ability to influence a positive outcome in our endeavors.

U.S. landpower forces have always proven themselves capable of operating in such a manner to "spare civilians from the effects of hostilities…strict compliance…with international humanitarian law and, in particular, with the principles of distinction and proportionality…while taking all feasible precautions in attack and defense."[42] We understand this, but to focus on our operating environment is not enough. We must now, more than ever, focus on the human domain. We have certainly invested much effort over the past decade to better understand what it means to secure populations. With the advent of the human domain, through the nexus of human security considerations and globalization, we must fully apply the myriad lessons we've learned and completely understand the advantage we'll be able to garner. This is particularly true outside major force-on-force conflict, today's wars, as we've come to fully grasp the significance of the protection of civilians, not defeating an enemy, is the end in itself that we'll most often seek to obtain.[43] We can, and will, do both. We live and operate within the human domain. Let's figure what that truly means, and how to best take advantage of the opportunities that have been presented us.

Endnotes

[1] U.S. Department of the Army, *Special Operations*, Army Doctrine Publication 3-05 (Washington, DC: U.S. Department of the Army, August 30, 2012), Foreword.

[2] U.S. Department of the Army, *The Army*, Army Doctrine Publication 1 (Washington, DC: U.S. Department of the Army, September 17, 2012), 1.

[3] Carl von Clausewitz, *On War*, trans. J.J. Graham, ed. F. N. Maude (London, England: N. Trubner, 1908), 53.

[4] Carl von Clausewitz, *On War*, trans. Michael Howard and Peter Paret (Princeton, NJ: Princeton University Press, 1976), 593.

[5] U.S. Department of the Army, *The Army*, Foreword.

[6] Ibid, 1-6.

[7] Rupert Smith, *The Utility of Force: The Art of War in the Modern World* (New York, NY: Vintage Books, Random House, 2005), 5.

[8] John M. McHugh and Raymond T. Odierno, *A Statement on the Posture of the United States Army 2012 to the Committees and Subcommittees of the United States Senate and House of Representatives,* Posture Statement presented to the 112th Congress, 2nd sess. (Washington, DC: U.S. Department of the Army, 2012), 1.

[9] United Nations General Assembly, *Follow-up to Paragraph 143 on Human Security of the 2005 World Summit Outcome* (New York, NY: United Nations, September 6, 2012), 1.

[10] Paul Heinbecker, "Human Security," *Behind the Headlines*, volume 56(2) (January-March 1999): 4-9.

[11] Paul Heinbecker, "The Concept of Human Security: A Canadian View," *Royal United Services Institute for Defence and Security Studies Journal,* no. 145.6 (Dec, 2000): 27-31.

[12] U.S. Joint Chiefs of Staff, *Irregular Warfare: Countering Irregular Threats,* Joint Operating Concept Version 2.0 (Washington, DC: U.S. Joint Chiefs of Staff, May, 17 2010), 4.

[13] Smith, *The Utility of Force*, x.

[14] U.S. Joint Chiefs of Staff, *Doctrine for the Armed Forces of the United States*, Joint Publication 1 Incorporating Change 1 (Washington, DC: U.S. Joint Chiefs of Staff, March 20, 2009), xii.

[15] U.S. Department of the Army, *The Army*, 1-4.

[16] Charles T. Cleveland, "Army Special Operations: Leading the Way in Human Domain Warfare," *ARMY,* Oct 2012, 62.

[17] Sun Tzu, *The Art of War*, trans. Samuel B. Griffith (New York: Oxford University Press, 1973), 98.

[18] Colin S. Gray, *Modern Strategy* (Oxford: Oxford University Press, 1999), quoted in U.S. Joint Chiefs of Staff, *Command and Control for Joint Land Operations,* Joint Publication 3-31 (Washington, DC: U.S. Joint Chiefs of Staff, June 29, 2010), I-4.

[19] Steven Metz, *"Strategic Horizons: U.S. Army Prepares for Human Domain of War,"* November 7, 2012, http://www.worldpoliticsreview.com/articles/12481/strategic-horizons-u-s-army-prepares-for-human-domain-of-war (accessed November 27, 2012).

[20] Barack Obama, *United States National Security Strategy* (Washington, DC: The White House, May 2010), 5.

[21] Phillip Killicoat, *"World Bank Policy Research Working Paper 4202,"* April 2007, http://www-wds.worldbank.org/servlet/WDSContentServer/WDSP/IB/2007/04/13/000016406 _20070413145045/Rendered/PDF/wps4202.pdf (accessed December 5, 2012).

[22] United Nations Security Council, "Report of the Secretary-General to the Security Council on the Protection of Civilians in Armed Conflict," (New York, NY: The United Nations, March 30, 2001), 14.

[23] Heinbecker, "The Concept of Human Security: A Canadian View," 2.

[24] Major General (ret.) Kees Homan, "The Military and Human Security," *Clingendael Institute Security and Human Rights Journal*, no. 1 (2008): 3.

[25] LTG Raymondo Ferrer, Armed Forces of the Philippines, Western Mindanao Command commanding general, interview by author, Zamboanga City, Mindanao, Philippines, June 2011.

[26] Bryony Lau, "South Philippines Best Chance for Peace," October 16, 2012, 1, http://www.crisisgroup.org/en/regions/asia/south-east-asia/philippines/lau-south-philippines-best-chance-for-peace.aspx (accessed October 21, 2012).

[27] U.S. Department of State, *The US Military Counterterrorism Campaign in 2002: A Summary* (Washington, DC: U.S. Department of State, November 28, 2012): 2-3.

[28] Geoffrey Lambert, Larry Lewis, and Sarah Sewall, "Operation Enduring Freedom—Philippines: Civilian Harm and the Indirect Approach," *Center for Complex Operations Prism 3*, no. 4 (September 2012): 4.

[29] Thomas Lum, *The Republic of the Philippines and U.S. Interests* (Washington, DC: U.S. Library of Congress, Congressional Research Service, January 3, 2011), 10.

[30] International Crisis Group, "The Philippines: Counter-insurgency vs. Counter-terrorism in Mindanao," International Crisis Group, May, 2008, 1, http://www.crisisgroup.org/en/regions/asia/south-east-asia/philippines/152-the-philippines-counter-insurgency-vs-counter-terrorism-in-mindanao.aspx (accessed August 26, 2012).

[31] Benigno S. Aquino III, *Foreword to Internal Peace and Security Plan "Bayanihan*, (Camp General Emilio Aquinaldo, Quezon City, Republic of the Philippines: Armed Forces of the Philippines, December 2010), i.

[32] Armed Forces of the Philippines, *Internal Peace and Security Plan "Bayanihan,"* (Camp General Emilio Aquinaldo, Quezon City, Republic of the Philippines: Armed Forces of the Philippines, December 2010), 1.

[33] Ibid., 2.

[34] President Benigno S. Aquino III, *Armed Forces of the Philippines Change of Command Ceremony Remarks* (Camp General Emilio Aquinaldo, Quezon City, Philippines, July 2, 2010), quoted in Armed Forces of the Philippines, *Internal Peace and Security Plan "Bayanihan,"* (Camp General Emilio Aquinaldo, Quezon City, Republic of the Philippines: Armed Forces of the Philippines, December 2010).

[35] Armed Forces of the Philippines, *Internal Peace and Security Plan "Bayanihan,"* 22.

[36] Colonel Charlie Galvez, "*IPSP "Bayanihan,"* briefing slide 20, Camp General Emilio Aquinaldo, Quezon City, Philippines, Office of the Deputy Chief of Staff for Operations, J3, General HQ, Armed Forces of the Philippines, May, 2012.

[37] Kofi Annan, *Secretary General Salutes International Workshop on Human Security in Mongolia* (Ulaanbaatar, Mongolia 08-10 May 2000), quoted in Armed Forces of the Philippines, *Internal Peace and Security Plan "Bayanihan,"* (Camp General Emilio Aquinaldo, Quezon City, Republic of the Philippines: Armed Forces of the Philippines, December, 2010), 26.

[38] Armed Forces of the Philippines, *Internal Peace and Security Plan "Bayanihan,"* 25.

[39] United States Joint Forces Command (J59) Joint Futures Group, *The Joint Operating Environment 2010*, (Norfolk, VA: February 18, 2010), 16.

[40] Lukas Milevski, "Fortissimus Inter Pares: The Utility of Landpower in Grand Strategy," *Parameters* 42, no. 2 (Summer 2012): 6.

[41] United Nations General Assembly, "Follow-up to paragraph 143 on human security of the 2005 World Summit Outcome," (New York, NY: The United Nations, September 6, 2012), 2.

[42] United Nations Security Council, "Report of the Secretary-General to the Security Council on the Protection of Civilians in Armed Conflict," (New York, NY: The United Nations, November 11, 2010), 10.

[43] Homan, "The Military and Human Security," 2.